Alone, She Sits

By Tracilyn George

Contents

SOUL SENSITIVE	4
VALUE THE MOMENT	5
AFTERMATH	7
I AM NOT AFRAID	8
COMPASSION	10
WOE IS ME	11
DARKEST HOUR	12
AWARENESS	14
TO NO AVAIL	16
ANOINTED	18
SOUL ASYLUM	20
TURMOIL	22
SHUT UP AND LISTEN	24
WHAT IF?	25
CONDEMNATION	28
ALONE, SHE SITS	29
ENRAPTURED	32
PARANOIA	33
ASYLUM	35
BE	37
SANCTUAERIE	38
HUMILITY	40
COMFORT IN CHAOS	41
SLAVE OF WORDS	43
THE DEMON	44
ABYSS	45
UNCOMMON	46
SHADOWS	47
EMPTY EYES	48
AFFECTION	49

SLEEP BECOMES ME 50
LOVE YOU GENTLY 52
DEMONS 54
NO ESCAPE 56

SOUL SENSITIVE

One body
Two souls
One soul to protect another.
A soul
So deep
So sensitive
Only few –
The kindred few –
Can detect it.
Soul searching soul
Searching solitude
Finding nothing
Wishing laughter
Granted tears.
Fears multiplied
Intensified
Deeply rooted
In the second soul
Damaged eternally
If weeded too fast.
Soul searching
Compromise.
Inner peace
Inner conflicts
Inner truce.
Call a ceasefire
Between the demons
If for only a moment
To catch
One's breath.

VALUE THE MOMENT

Peace inside
Peace without
Value the moment
Each and every one
For they are few
And far between.
Joy within
Joy surrounds
Value the moment
Each and every one
For they are rare
And they are fleeting.
Love intense
Love unlimited
Value the moment
Each and every one
For they are pure
And they are precious.
Anger rising
Anger flaring
Value the moment
Each and every one
For they define
And they refresh.
Sadness lingers
Sadness fingers
Value the moment
Each and every one
For they are brief
And they are gifts.
Peace inside
Peace without

Value the moment
Each and every one
For they are few
And far between.

AFTERMATH

Darkness comes
No will to live
Unending depression
No crying
No laughing
Nothing
Emotionless
Staring into space
Silent pleas for help
No one hears
For no one cares
Deeper and deeper
I fall into myself
I reach out
But no one's around
Death makes sense
No fear
No pain
Farewell
Forever

I AM NOT AFRAID

I am not afraid
For you are here
With your arms
So strong
So comforting
Holding me close.
I am not afraid
For you are here
With your eyes
So kind
So gentle
Easing my pain.
I am not afraid
For you are here
With your voice
So soft
So soothing
Comforting my soul.
I am not afraid
For you are here
With your touch
So light
Enticing
Setting me free.
I am not afraid
For you are here
With your smile
So bright
So sweet
I am content.
I am not afraid
For you are here

Doing what
You do best
Loving me
Unconditionally
And by loving me
I am not afraid.

COMPASSION

Extend a hand.
Lend an ear.
Be quiet
And listen.
Show some compassion.
Give a hug.
Show a smile.
Be silent and
Pay attention.
Show some compassion.
Ask questions.
Listen carefully.
Be quiet
And hear.
Show some compassion.
Be open
And willing.
Be silent
And see.
Show some compassion.

WOE IS ME

My heart, it breaks.
It cannot see.
Can you hear?
Oh, woe is me.
My eyes, they cry.
They are in need.
Are you here?
Oh, woe is me.
My lips, they quiver
Yet they cannot speak.
Are you here?
Oh, woe is me.
My legs, they shake.
They are not free.
Are you near?
Oh, woe is me.
My body is numb.
It cannot feel
Because you are not here.
Oh, woe is me.

DARKEST HOUR

Let me see you through
Your darkest hour.
Let me show you all
Of my heart's desire.
Let me see you through
Your darkest hour.
Babe, it has to be
Now or never.
Let me take you on
A midnight cruise,
Walk along the beach
Without our shoes.
Let me hold you warmly
By the fire.
Let me satisfy
Your deepest desire.
Let me see you through
Your darkest hour.
Let me show you all
Of my heart's desire.
Let me see you through
Your darkest hour.
Babe, it has to be
Now or never.
I'm tell you from my
Heart of hearts
That I hope we
Will never part.
To know that you really
Love me, dear
Would be the greatest thing
I could ever hear.

Let me see you through
Your darkest hour.
Let me show you all
Of my heart's desire.
Let me see you through
Your darkest hour.
Babe, it has to be
Now or never.
Let me help you to
Forget the pain.
You know I'll be there for you
Again and again.
Let me show you what it is
To be in love.
What's in your heart
And soul's enough.
Let me see you through
Your darkest hour.
Let me show you all
Of my heart's desire.
Let me see you through
Your darkest hour.
Babe, it has to be
Now or never.

AWARENESS

Look around you;
See what is going on
Around you.
Pay attention
To the little things.
Examine the details
Then step back
And see the big picture.
Be aware
Of your surroundings.
Be cognizant
Of those around you.
In silence,
You see more
Hear more
Feel more.
Learn to listen.
Learn to not speak.
Learn to see.
Learn to feel.
Be aware
Of who you are
And how you are perceived.
Learn why you do
What you do
But you need
To be quiet
Long enough;
Alone
Long enough
To examine
Who you are

And how you lived
Your life.
It is time
To become aware
Of your decisions
Both good and bad
And how that affects you
In the present.

TO NO AVAIL

She shakes
Shivering
In pain
Wishing
Begging
For it to
Just go away
To no avail.
She walks
Alone
Misery
Etched upon
Her worn
Tired face.
Her eyes
Pleading
To those
She passes to help her.
She cries
Alone
In her room
In hopes
To release
The heartache
But to no avail.
Desperate
She is
To find the way
To escape
The agony
To no avail.
Her soul

In despair
Crying
To be heard
To no avail.
Her mind
It wanders
In and out
Of nightmares.
Dreams
So horrific
No normal person
Could survive them
Yet she goes on
Shaking
Shivering
In pain
Wishing
Begging
For it to
Just go away
To no avail.

ANOINTED
Follow
The single ray
Of sunshine
And you will
Find him
The anointed one.
He
Is the one
To save us all.
He
Is calm
In the face
Of adversity.
He
Is the safe haven
From the storm.
He
Is the one
The anointed one.
He
Is the one
To provide comfort
In chaotic times.
He
Will hold you
In times of need.
He
Is the one
The anointed one.
He
Will show you
What true love is.

He
Will keep you
From total darkness
And despair.
He
Is the one
The anointed one.

SOUL ASYLUM

Come inside.
See what I see
Every day
Every night
Come experience
The nightmare I live
Every waking moment
Every restless night.
Come feel the pain
The hatred
The anger.
Can you feel it?
Do you understand?
Come deal with the repulsion,
The desire to rid of it.
The weight upon your chest
Welling up to your throat.
Take a tour in my world.
Feel the torment
The taunting
The rage.
See what only I see
When I look into the glass.
Bear the ugliness
Beneath the surface.
Can you stand it?
Live the darkness
Within my being.
Can you take it?
Dig within my soul.
Do you think
You can go that low?

Find the trail
To the reason.
Follow to the why.
Be not afraid to cry.
Wash away the guilt.
My foundation will be built
Amongst the chaos
And the rubble.
I will triumph over trouble.
I have before.
I will again.
Don't you worry,
My good friend.
My time will come
When I shall rise
To see what you see
Through my eyes.

TURMOIL
Silence falls
Crashing to the earth
Like a wayward comet
That has lost its way.
In the corner
I sit
Alone in the darkness
Yet not alone in my thinking.
I cry
But yet I do not.
I cannot show it.
I scream
Yell
But no one hears.
No one understands
My turmoil.
No one could.
Only those
Who share in my misery
Understand
The need to let
Everything go
To cry
For nothing
To scream
For naught.
To unleash the terror
The weight
Upon my shoulders
Overwhelming
I cannot bear it
But yet

I must
For I cannot
Burden others
With my turmoil
For it is
Not their cross
But mine
To bear.
Only those
Who share in my misery
Truly understand
The need
To cry
To scream
To release
The turmoil.

SHUT UP AND LISTEN
Stop talking
And listen
To what is
Not being said.
Hear beyond the words.
Shut up
Stop listening
To the sound
Of your own voice.
Be quiet
Long enough
To dig beneath
The surface.
Try to understand
To what
You are being told.
Find out
What is beyond
The words.
Watch the
Body language.
The eyes will
Tell you everything
You need to know.
Shut up
And listen –
Truly listen –
To what is
Not being said.

WHAT IF?

What if
We were all equal?
Men and women
People of all colors
And religions?
What if
We didn't judge
Solely upon
Outward appearances?
What if
We approached others
With genuine interest
Instead of idle curiosity?
What if
We smile more
Instead of frowns
And scowls on
A regular basis?
What if
We heard others more
Instead of listening
To the sound
Of our own voice?
What if
We allowed ourselves
To imagine more?
Believe in ideas
Bigger than ourselves?
What if
We allowed our children
To believe they
Can do whatever

They put their minds
In achieving?
What if
We didn't rain
On the parade of others?
What if
We were positive
About everything
Surrounding us?
What if
We eliminated
The negative images
We are persistently
Bombarded with
On a daily basis?
What if
There was peace
Among nations
Or even
Amongst ourselves?
What if
We believed
In our abilities
To change the world
For the better?
What if
We no longer
Allowed others
To dictate to us
How we should live
Our lives?
What if
We always did

What was right
Regardless
Of the outcome
Or the potential
Retaliation?
What if
We were no longer
Afraid
Of other people?
Think
Of the possibilities
We can perform
If we were all
Permitted the
What if.

CONDEMNATION

Grey skies loom
Heavily overhead
Ominously whispering
Their words of condemnation.
Wild winds whistle
Through threadbare trees
Screaming sinister threats
And uttering their condemnation.
Dogs, once dormant
Wail forlornly
In the distance
Howling menacingly
Their views and condemnation.
Feral cats hiss
Screeching hatefully
In run-down alleys
Squealing hideously
Their sneers and condemnation.
Birds of prey
Soar as the unsavory vultures they are
Squawking loudly
Lying in wait
To spew their condemnation.

ALONE, SHE SITS

Alone, she sits
Lost
In her thoughts.
Pain
Simmering
To a boil
Inside her.
Frustrated,
She screams
In hopes
Of setting free
The time bomb
Ticking
Quickly
Quietly
Within her.
But her screams
Do no good.
The pressure
Increases
To where
She cannot
Breathe.
She cries
In anguish –
Lost
In despair.
So far gone
Is she
She cannot
Find her
Way back.

Alone
She is
Within a crowd
Surrounded
By herself.
Her head
Spinning
Thoughts
Of hopelessness
Helplessness
Fill her mind.
Her heart
Weighted
By the chains
Of her soul.
She sits
Alone
Lost
In her thoughts,
Afraid
Of the hurt,
Unsure
Of where
It is leading her.
She shivers
Shakes
Trembling with fear,
Hating herself
And those
Around her;
No understanding
Why they
Do not listen.

Alone
She sits
Lost
In her thoughts,
Believing
Her demons
Whispering
About her,
Pointing out
Her flaws
Her minor
Imperfections.
She sits
Alone
Her head
In her hands,
Sobbing
But fall no tears.
She begs
Pleads
For an end
To the pain.
She hears
But nothing
So alone
She sits
Lost
In thought.

ENRAPTURED

Eyes glazed
Enchanted.
Face flushed
Embarrassed.
Hands trembled
Excited.
Heart fluttered
Enraptured.
Lip bitten
Intrigued.
Giggles escaped
Anxious.
Body quivered
Anticipated.
Smile transfixed
Elated.
Fingers caressed
Adored.
Hair entwined
Enamored.
Eyes glazed
Enraptured.

PARANOIA

On the inside
Looking out
All around you
Enemies sit
Preparing to pounce
In a moment
Of weakness.
Nerves a-bundled
On the edge
Cannot sit
Cannot flee
The enemies hide
In every crevice
Ready to attack
At a moment's notice.
Enemies everywhere
Constantly on the lookout
For an instant
Of weakness
Playing games
With a busy head
Barrage non-stop
To maintain control
Fury flurries
Through an unstable soul
Imagined enemies
All around
Attacking from the outside
Encouraged from the inside.
Raging voices
Scream incessantly
Reinforcing the demons

Already toying
With the mind.
Nothing helps
To end the onslaught
For the enemies
Are everywhere
Preparing to pounce
In a moment
Of weakness.

ASYLUM

In this dark
And dismal world,
I seek refuge
From the madness.
I search for someone
To calm me
And ease
My increasing pain.
Is there anyone
Out there
Who can hear me
And answer my pleas?
Sanctuary!
Sanctuary!
Please,
Somebody
Give me sanctuary!
My soul is aching
And my heart is wanting!
Emptiness
Controls my life.
I crave
The comforting arms
Of another
But my hopes
Are so low
I doubt
He will ever
Find his way
Into my life.
Even if he did,
I am so decrepit

He would continue
To just pass on by –
And look for
Someone better;
Someone without
The weight of the world
Upon her shoulders.
Asylum!
Please, someone
Find me asylum!
Show me the way
To emotional freedom.
Lead me to the one
Who can free me
From my jail cell.
I need sanctuary!
I need it soon
Before I die
A long and painful death.

BE

Be not a person of success but one of value.
Be a person who enriches the lives of others.
Be a person who knows who you are.
Be a person who knows what you want.
Be a person of destiny.
Be a person of courage.
Be a person who aims high and far.
Be a person of confidence.
Be a person who fulfills their vision.
Be a person who overcomes.
Be a person of action.
Be a person who always does what is right.
Be a person who never gives up.
But most importantly,
Be legendary!

SANCTUAERIE

In his arms
I will find
My sanctuaerie
So strong
So warm
They comfort me
When I am distraught.
In his eyes
I will find
My sanctuaerie
So kind
So caring
They calm me
When I am distressed.
In his smile
I will find
My sanctuaerie
So bright
So loving
It softens me
When I've been hardened.
In his fingers
I will find
My sanctuaerie
So light
So tender
They let me know
I am loved.
In his arms
I will find
My sanctuaerie
So strong

So warm
They comfort me
When I am distraught.

HUMILITY

Her face flushes
Embarrassed by the accolades.
Her eyes fall
Unaccustomed to the praise
For she does
Her good deeds
For the simple act
Of giving.
She smiles shyly
Under the scrutiny
Of those who choose
To be blind
To how true living
Really is about.
Others are humbled
By her generosity
Without thought
Of reciprocity.
She is humbled
By the gratitude
Received from those
She gave of herself.

COMFORT IN CHAOS

Calm drives you crazy
For it gives you
Time to think
Thoughts running rampant
Destroying your head and
Killing your spirit.
But you find
Comfort in chaos
For it keeps you
On your toes.
There is no time to stop
To evaluate your choices or
To second-guess your life.
Calm drives you crazy
For you don't know
What to do.
You can't appreciate the silence
Bringing about peace and
Quieting your pain.
But you find
Comfort in chaos
For it keeps you
On your toes.
There is no time to stop
To evaluate your choices or
To second-guess your life.
Calm drives you crazy
For it opens
Up your mind
Sending in ideas
To shock you into living and
To open up your world.

But you find
Comfort in chaos
For it keeps you
On your toes.
There is no time to stop
To evaluate your choices or
To second-guess your life.

SLAVE OF WORDS

How dare you say
Feelings are not real?
Does that make you not real?
If you are not feeling –
You are not living.
Would you say
Thoughts are not real?
Just because they
Are not tangible
It does not make them invalid.
Embrace your feelings;
Take hold of your thoughts
For they are as real as you are.
When you stop feeling
When you stop thinking
You stop being.

THE DEMON

The demon lurking
In shadows hiding
Preparing to pounce
In a moment
Of vulnerability.
The demon seething
Paranoia
Pounding mistruths
Upon an already
Distrusting mind.
The demon screeching
Taking over
Mind manipulating
Turning others
Into the enemy.
The demon prowling
Flaring nostrils
Voices snarling
Taunting
Continuously.
The demon creeping
Footsteps pounding
Whispers screaming
Bombarding
Angry untruths.
The demon lurking
In shadows hiding
Preparing to pounce
In a moment
Of vulnerability.

ABYSS

Darkness plunging
Making way
For anger.
Emotions raging
Drawing you under.
Hatred seething
Through your veins
Lashing out
To vent frustration.
Pain embedded
Deep in your soul
Silent screaming
Fills the air.
You crave affection
But no one cares.
Heavy weights
Inhibit breathing.
Tears that linger
But do not fall.
Under attack
From every angle.
No peace in sight.
It is elusive
Plunging darkness
Into the abyss.

UNCOMMON

When did love
Become so uncommon?
Why is hatred
So prevalent in our lives?
When did compassion
Become so uncommon?
Why is seeking revenge
So important to our psyches?
When did kindness
Become so uncommon?
Why is anger
So embedded in our souls?
When did laughter
Become so uncommon?
Why is sadness
So ingrained in our heads?
When did serenity
Become so uncommon?
Why is upheaval
So rampant in our world?
When did selflessness
Become so uncommon?
Why is egotism
So limitless in our being?
When did love
Become so uncommon?
Why are we so afraid
To let it into our lives?

SHADOWS

Demons raise
Their ugly heads
Imposing their will
Upon the vulnerable
And the unsuspecting.
They flare their nostrils
Sinister and unrelenting
Intimidating those
That will listen.
Their shadows defy you
To remain unafraid.
Their eyes piercing
Through a fragile soul.
Shrieks unyielding
Penetrating one's being.
Anger raging
Multiplying
As it pummels its way
Through the masses.
Demons unleash
Their voodoo
Upon those
Without defenses
Strong enough
To withstand
The onslaught.

EMPTY EYES

Always watching
But never seeing.
Always listening
But never hearing.
Always knowing
But never feeling.
Always stating
But never thinking.
Always spouting
But never believing.
Always searching
But never looking.
Always wanting
But never giving.
Always needing
But never having.
Always craving
But never yearning.
Always demanding
But never loving.
Always reaching
But never holding.
Empty eyes are
Always void
For empty eyes
Reveal the nothing
Within the soul.

AFFECTION

Arms outstretching
Warm embrace
Eyes aglitter
Love enraptured
Fingers caressing
Calming affect
Hands cupping
A haggard face
Smiling warmly
To ease the mind.
Giggles escaping
Breaking the tension
Kisses soft
Upon the forehead
Faces blushing
At loving glances
Affection flowing
Without boundaries.
Softness lingers
Amidst the harshness
Quieting doubts
Encouraging trust
Arms embracing
To comfort thee.

SLEEP BECOMES ME

I walk
Alone
Along the crowded streets
Unaware
Uncaring
Of the goings-on
Around me.
The numbing pain
In my body
Consumes me
Overtakes my attention.
I want
So badly
To sleep
But my body
Keeps wandering
Aimlessly
Through unknowing streets
Past uncaring souls.
My pace
Becoming painstakingly
Slower with
Every step.
It seems
Minutes are days
Days – weeks.
My heart
Not in it
As it used to be.
I feel my body
Becoming lighter.
I am so tired,

I fall
Upon the cold
Wet pavement as
Sleep
Becomes me.

LOVE YOU GENTLY

Let me love you gently
Through the night
Show you a world
Beyond your eyes
Let me love you gently
Through the night
It's time for you to see
What I can see
Come to my arms
My precious one
Come to the arms
So strong and warm
Where else in the world
Can you find someone?
Who will keep you safe?
From nature's harm
Let me love you gently
Through the night
Show you a world
Beyond your eyes
Let me love you gently
Through the night
It's time for you to see
What I can see
Stop and take another
Look around
Think and then tell me
What you have found
What you see is
What you feel
Let my love for you
Help you heal

Let me love you gently
Through the night
Show you a world
Beyond your eyes
Let me love you gently
Through the night
It's time for you to see
What I can see
Let me show you
How to love again
Show you what it's like
To have a man
Not like the boys
You used to have
But a gentleman
Who won't treat you bad?
Let me love you gently
Through the night
Show you a world
Beyond your eyes
Let me love you gently
Through the night
It's time for you to see
What I can see

DEMONS

Eyes
Smoky green
Turn emerald
In the moonlight.
Flushed cheeks
On an ivory face
Revealing conquered demons within.
A troubled soul
Searching
Relentlessly
For peace.
Her minds
Racing
From heartache
To heartbreak
Never escaping
Never breaking through
The darkness.
Trying
And failing
To free herself
From the torment
Unknowing
Of the feeling
Of being ahead
Of the game.
Every step forward
Is pushed back two
Fighting the losing battle
For footing
On solid ground.
Her body

'Though solid
Is unsteady
Too weak
At times
To aid the war
Against the demons
Within
And monsters
Without.

NO ESCAPE

Darkness inches
Towards the soul
Overtaking
Every bit
Of lit
It still possesses;
Working its way
Toward the mind
Taking control
Of the senses
As it does so.
You want to scream
But no sound escapes.
You want to cry
But no tears emerge.
You try to fight
The inner battle
But learn
It is a losing effort
For there is no escape
From the darkness
Which consumes
Your body
Your mind
Your soul.

www.ingramcontent.com/pod-product-compliance
Lightning Source LLC
LaVergne TN
LVHW090039080526
838202LV00046B/3882